Searchlight Books

The Kids' Guide to Government

How Checks and Balances Work

Zelda Wagner

Lerner Publications ◆ Minneapolis

Copyright © 2025 by Lerner Publishing Group, Inc.

All rights reserved. International copyright secured. No part of this book may be reproduced, stored in a retrieval system, or transmitted in any form or by any means—electronic, mechanical, photocopying, recording, or otherwise—without the prior written permission of Lerner Publishing Group, Inc., except for the inclusion of brief quotations in an acknowledged review.

Lerner Publications Company
An imprint of Lerner Publishing Group, Inc.
241 First Avenue North
Minneapolis, MN 55401 USA

For reading levels and more information, look up this title at www.lernerbooks.com.

Main body text set in Adrianna Regular.
Typeface provided by Chank.

Library of Congress Cataloging-in-Publication Data

Names: Wagner, Zelda, 2000– author.
Title: How checks and balances work / Zelda Wagner.
Description: Minneapolis : Lerner Publications, 2025. | Series: Searchlight books. The kids' guide to government | Includes bibliographical references and index. | Audience: Ages 8–11 | Audience: Grades 4–6 | Summary: "From a president's veto to a Supreme Court decision on a law, young readers learn all about checks and balances in the US government. Discover how checks and balances help the US stay a democracy"— Provided by publisher.
Identifiers: LCCN 2023035572 (print) | LCCN 2023035573 (ebook) | ISBN 9798765626573 (library binding) | ISBN 9798765629604 (paperback) | ISBN 9798765637081 (epub)
Subjects: LCSH: Separation of powers—United States—Juvenile literature. | United States—Politics and government—Juvenile literature.
Classification: LCC JK305 .W34 2025 (print) | LCC JK305 (ebook) | DDC 320.473/04—dc23/eng/20230807

LC record available at https://lccn.loc.gov/2023035572
LC ebook record available at https://lccn.loc.gov/2023035573

Manufactured in the United States of America
1-1009925-51988-10/4/2023

Table of Contents

Chapter 1
CHECKS AND BALANCES ... 4

Chapter 2
THE LEGISLATIVE BRANCH ... 12

Chapter 3
THE JUDICIAL BRANCH ... 19

Chapter 4
THE EXECUTIVE BRANCH ... 24

What Do You Think? • 29
Glossary • 30
Learn More • 31
Index • 32

Chapter 1

CHECKS AND BALANCES

In 2023, the Supreme Court released its decision on President Joseph Biden's student debt plan. Many people in the United States have student debt from going to college. This is money usually owed to the US government or banks. Biden created a plan to help get rid of or lower the amount of money people owed. Six of the Supreme Court justices said that the president didn't have the power to lower people's debt. Three of the justices said that the president did. Since most of the justices decided against the plan, it ended.

The Supreme Court is a big part of the judicial branch. It is the highest court in the US. The president is part of the executive branch. Congress is the legislative branch. When the Supreme Court said no to Biden's student debt plan, it was an example of how checks and balances work between the three branches of government.

People protest the Supreme Court's decision to end Biden's student debt plan.

In a representative democracy, people vote for their leaders.

The Three Branches

The founders of the United States wanted to create a system where people had a say in their government. This type of government is called a democracy. In a democratic government, the people vote for who they want to represent them and make decisions for the country. The founders created a system of checks and balances using the three branches of US government. Each branch has its own jobs. Some of these jobs are checking on the other branches. Then they can make sure each branch is equal and one doesn't become more powerful than the others.

The legislative branch is made up of the House of Representatives and the Senate. This branch is also called Congress. Members of Congress are chosen by US citizens that are eighteen years old or older. Congress's main job is to create laws.

Congress meets at the US Capitol in Washington, DC.

Federal courts, including the Supreme Court, are the judicial branch. The judicial branch makes sure the Constitution is followed. It decides court cases based on its understanding of the Constitution.

THE SUPREME COURT HEARS AND DECIDES CASES.

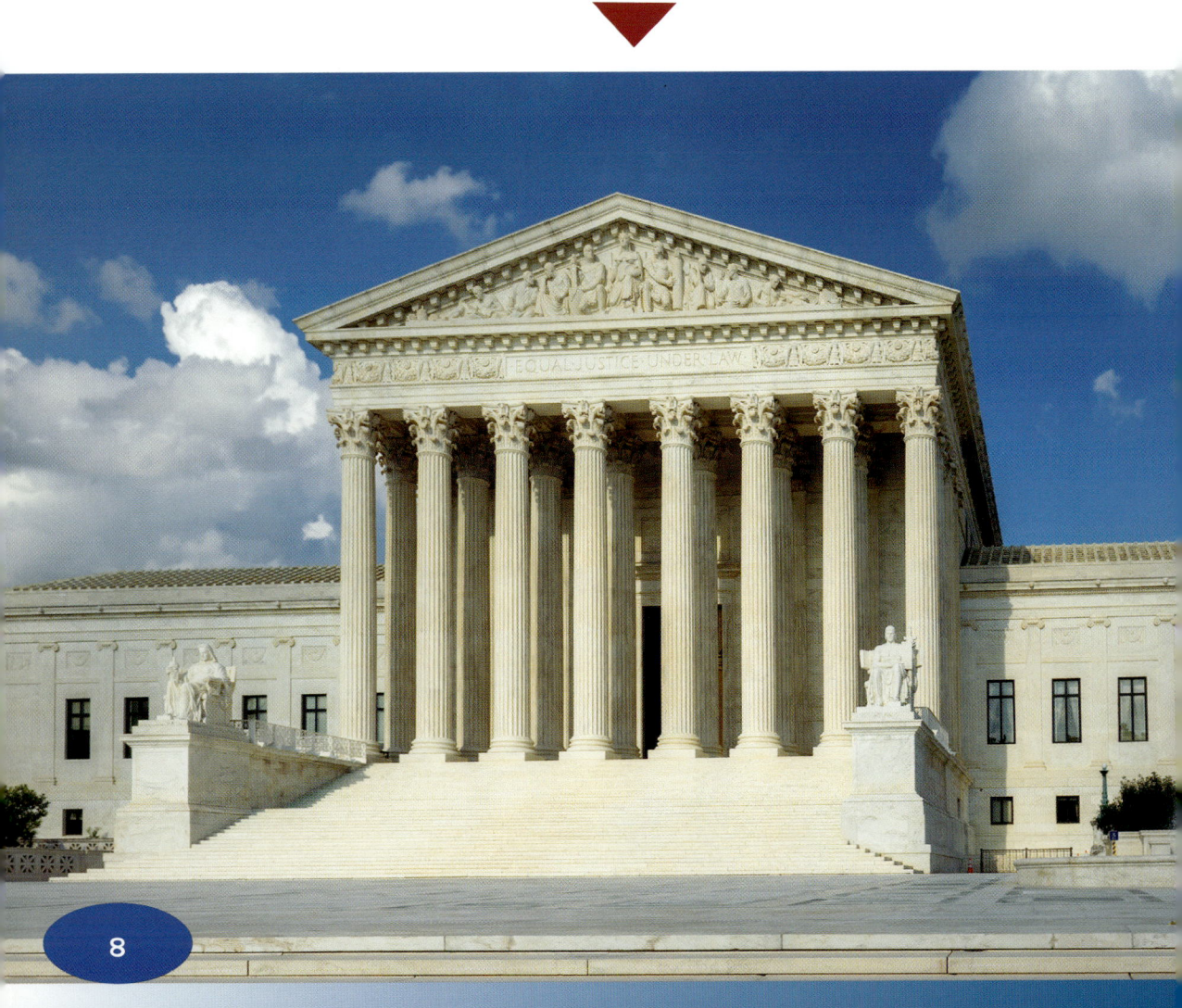

Democracy and You

Checks and balances aren't just for the government. They are all around you. These checks and balances make sure things are fair. At some major sporting events, refs watch players to make sure rules are followed. If a coach doesn't agree with their decision, they can challenge it. Then someone from the league looks at the play and makes a decision. Where else in your life do you see checks and balances? Do you see them at your school or at home?

The executive branch includes the president, vice president, and other offices. This branch carries out laws made by the legislative branch. The executive branch makes sure laws are followed.

Vice President Kamala Harris gives a speech in 2023.

House minority leader Hakeem Jeffries (*left*) and Speaker of the House Kevin McCarthy (*right*) talk in 2023.

Working Together

Checks and balances make sure that the branches of government work together. For example, the House and the Senate work together to create and pass bills. If they pass a bill, it goes to the president who can then sign or veto it. If Congress can't agree on a bill, the bill will not be passed. Then it doesn't go to the president.

Chapter 2

THE LEGISLATIVE BRANCH

The legislative branch makes laws, but it also has checks it can do. The legislative branch can impeach people in the other branches. This means it can charge the president or Supreme Court justices with a formal accusation if they don't follow the rules.

Senate majority leader Mitch McConnell talks during a 2021 hearing.

SEN. McCONNELL

Checking the Executive Branch

The executive branch can veto bills. It can say no to a bill passed by Congress. If Congress doesn't agree with the president's decision, it can still move the bill forward. This means a bill can pass even if the president vetoes it. But Congress needs to have a vote. Two-thirds of the House and the Senate have to vote for the bill. If they do, then it passes. This is different from when Congress normally passes bills to the president. In that case, they only need more than half of the House and the Senate to vote for it.

The legislative branch helps decide who will be in the executive branch. Congress must approve all the president's cabinet members, or advisers, before they can start their jobs. The Senate approves who the president chooses to be US ambassadors to other countries.

REPRESENTATIVE DEB HAALAND SPEAKS AT A HEARING BEFORE JOINING THE CABINET.

Speaker McCarthy (*left*) and President Biden (*right*) talk about the federal budget in 2023.

Congress also decides if it will approve the president's yearly budget for the nation. The president gives ideas on how to spend the federal budget, but they can't approve it. Congress makes the final decision.

Congress has the power to declare war. This helps it check the president. The president leads the military as commander in chief. But they need approval from Congress before starting or joining a war.

Checking the Judicial Branch

With the president's approval, Congress can change the number of justices on the Supreme Court. It can offer amendments, or changes, to the Constitution. Congress also has the power to change or clarify laws that the judicial branch said were unconstitutional.

Congress has to vote to change or clarify laws.

Deep Dive

Senators represent their state. Each state sends two senators to Congress. Each state has at least one representative in the House. The number of representatives is decided by the number of people who live in that state. Smaller states such as Vermont and Delaware have one representative. Bigger states have more representatives. A lot of people live in California, so they have fifty-two representatives.

Checking Itself

The House and the Senate check each other. Both parts of Congress have to agree before a bill passes. If the House wants a bill passed and the Senate decides not to pass it, the bill does not pass. The House also has this power over the Senate.

Senator Marco Rubio asks questions in a 2021 hearing.

Chapter 3

THE JUDICIAL BRANCH

Like Congress, the judicial branch has jobs that the other branches do not have. This branch checks the legislative branch by looking over passed bills. It checks the executive branch too. The president can sign a bill into law, and the judicial branch can decide it doesn't go along with the Constitution.

Checking the Executive Branch

The president places justices on the Supreme Court, but the president can't fire a justice. After a justice joins the court, they have their seat for life or until they retire. If the president is being impeached, the chief justice of the Supreme Court watches the trial. The chief justice is the justice in charge of the Supreme Court. Usually, the vice president is president of the Senate. The chief justice takes over because the vice president might stop the trial to help the president. The justice makes sure the trial continues.

There are nine justices on the Supreme Court.

Ketanji Brown Jackson (*left*) is sworn in as a Supreme Court justice in 2022.

Checking the Legislative Branch

The judicial branch also checks Congress when a president is being impeached. The court watches the Senate during an impeachment trial. The judicial branch can also look at laws Congress passes. It can say that a law is unconstitutional. Then the law ends after they give their ruling.

Supreme Court chief justice John Roberts speaks during President Donald Trump's impeachment trial in 2020.

Checking Itself

The judicial branch checks itself. For example, the Supreme Court has an odd number of judge seats. This makes sure decisions don't end up in a tie. The Supreme Court can also look at decisions they made in the past. They might decide that they were wrong in that decision and change it.

Deep Dive

The Constitution doesn't say how many justices are on the Supreme Court. In 1937 President Franklin Delano Roosevelt helped write a bill to increase the number of justices. His programs kept getting struck down by the Supreme Court, so he wanted new justices who would vote in his favor. But then the court began ruling with Roosevelt and the bill didn't pass.

Some people think that the Supreme Court should have more justices so that it will be more balanced. Others worry that the Supreme Court will just keep growing. What do you think?

Chapter 4

THE EXECUTIVE BRANCH

The executive branch deals with everyday life. It helps fund your local post office or police department. You might see a framed photo of the president in these places.

Checking the Legislative Branch

The president can check Congress by vetoing bills. That means that the executive branch can try to stop a bill Congress has passed from becoming a law.

Biden vetoes a bill in 2023.

Only the president can call Congress to an emergency meeting. This happens when a big decision needs to be made quickly. The president is the commander in chief of the army, navy, and other military services. If the president wants to go to war, they would call an emergency meeting.

Checking the Judicial Branch

The executive branch checks the judicial branch by nominating Supreme Court justices. When a seat on the court opens up, the president chooses someone who would be a good fit for the job. Then the Senate asks the person questions. After, they decide if they want to confirm the person or not. Similar to the president's cabinet members, anyone the president suggests for a job needs to be approved by Congress.

Judge Neil Gorsuch (*left*) speaks after being nominated by Trump in 2017.

A 2023 CABINET AND WHITE HOUSE SENIOR STAFF MEETING

Checking Itself

Like the other branches, the executive branch checks itself. The vice president and the cabinet make sure the president can do their job. They also ensure that the president is doing what is best for people in the US. If they decide the president can't do their job or isn't doing it well, they can remove the president. If that happens, the vice president would become president.

The US government has a system of checks and balances. This makes sure that the three branches have their own powers.

All three branches of government are located in the nation's capital, Washington, DC.

What Do You Think?

Those in favor of checks and balances argue that it maintains democracy. But some who question it believe the responsibilities of each branch of government overlap too much. They might say that it's not a true democracy. They may even say it opens the country up to conflict over which branch should be doing what.

Do you think the checks and balances system is working? Why or why not?

Glossary

ambassador: the highest-ranking person who represents their own government while living in another country

bill: a proposed law

budget: a yearly plan for how the US government will spend money

confirm: to give official approval

Constitution: a set of principles that established the US government

federal: relating to the United States' national government

impeach: to charge a public official with a crime

justice: a judge on the Supreme Court

nominate: to formally choose someone as a candidate for a job

Supreme Court: the highest and most powerful court in the US

trial: a formal meeting in a court where arguments are made to a judge and often a jury so that a decision can be made according to the law

unconstitutional: not consistent with the US Constitution

veto: to reject a bill

Learn More

Britannica Kids: Checks and Balances
https://kids.britannica.com/students/article/checks-and-balances/630952

Ducksters: US Government Checks and Balances
https://www.ducksters.com/history/us_government/checks_and_balances.php

Kenney, Karen Latchana. *Checks and Balances*. Minneapolis: Bearport, 2022.

Kids in the House: What Is Congress?
https://kids-clerk.house.gov/young-learners/lesson.html?intID=29

Rajczak, Michael. *What Are Checks and Balances?* New York: Gareth Stevens, 2022.

Wagner, Zelda. *How the Executive Branch Works*. Minneapolis: Lerner Publications, 2025.

Index

bills, 11, 13, 19, 24

Congress, 5, 7, 11, 13–19, 21, 24–26

executive branch, 5, 10, 13–14, 19–20, 24, 26–27

federal budget, 15

House of Representatives, 7, 11, 13–14, 17–18

impeachment, 21

judical branch, 5, 8, 16, 19, 21–22, 26

legislative branch, 5, 7, 10, 12, 14, 19, 21

Senate, 7, 11, 13–14, 18, 20–21, 26

Supreme Court, 4–5, 8, 12, 16, 20, 22–23, 26

veto, 11, 13, 24

Photo Acknowledgments

Image credits: Kevin Dietsch/Getty Images, p. 5; Michael Ciaglo/Getty Images, p. 6; Getty Images, p. 7; Lucky-photographer/Shutterstock, p. 8; Lawrence Jackson/The White House, p. 10; Tom Williams/CQ Roll Call via AP Images, p. 11; Al Drago/Bloomberg via Getty Images, p. 13; Sarah Silbiger-Pool/Getty Images, pp. 14, 18; SAUL LOEB/AFP via Getty Images, p. 15; Francis Chung/POLITICO via AP Images, p. 16; AP Photo/J. Scott Applewhite, p. 20; Fred Schilling/Collection of the Supreme Court of the United States via AP, p. 21; Senate Television via AP, p. 22; Adam Schulz/The White House, pp. 25, 27; AP Photo/Carolyn Kaster, p. 26; vichie81/Shutterstock, p. 28.

Cover: Kevin Dietsch/Getty Images; AP Photo/J. Scott Applewhite.